War, Refugees' Human Rights and World Peace

Akram Mohammad

Dedication

To my beloved late parents, Father Major M. Mustafa (Retired Indian Army Officer) and Mother Mrs. Kulsoom Begum, who planted the seed of knowledge in my mind and nurtured it. They instilled in me the belief that "words have the power to change the world.

I deeply cherish and profoundly miss the guidance, inspiration, and unwavering support of my late brother, Dr. M. Mukarram, Ph.D. (Aligarh Muslim University), and my late father-in-law, Dr. M. Shoeb Alam Khan, CMO, MBBS, MD. Additionally, I fondly remember my late sister, Mrs. Nasimun Nisa Farhat, BA, B.Ed. (Aligarh Muslim University), MA (Bananas Hindus University), who also contributed to shaping my life.

Their legacies continue to influence and inspire me every day.

Acknowledgment

I, Dr. Akram Mohammad, Ph.D. in Chemistry and LL.M., am profoundly grateful to my family for their unwavering encouragement and support in all my endeavors, inspiring me to pursue my dreams relentlessly. My heartfelt thanks go to my wife, Mrs. Nuzhat Alam Akram, B.A., who has been my pillar of strength, providing both emotional and financial support, without which completing this book would not have been possible.

I am immensely proud of my daughters and sons, each contributing their unique talents and support along this journey. Miss Afreenish Yusirah Akram, with her Bachelor's degree in Food Science and M.A. from Carleton University, Ottawa; Miss Parihan Israh Akram, who has pursued a Bachelor's degree in Health Science from Carleton University, Ottawa; and Miss Afrah Inshirah Akram, currently excelling in grade 5. Not forgetting my sons: Azfar Al-Affan Akram, with a Bachelor's degree in Biotechnology and M.Sc. from the University of Ottawa; Yawar Az-Farhan Akram, pursuing a Bachelor's degree in Biotechnology at the University of Ottawa; Zafar Eshan Akram, studying Neuroscience at Carleton University; and Uzair Ziad Akram, making strides in grade 12.

I extend my gratitude to my family members in India, particularly my brothers: Col. Dr. M. Azam, M.D., Ph.D.; Dr. M. Muazzam, M.Tech., Ph.D.; Prof. Dr. M. Aslam-Hameshgul, MD; Principal M. Samiullah, M.Com.; M. Ibrar Ahmed, M.A.; and Capt. Sabir Mahmood Khan.

Thanks are also due to my mother-in-law, Mrs. Najma Khatoon, my sisters-in-law, Mrs. Rafat Alam and Mrs. Farhat Alam, and my brother-in-law, Intekhab Alam. I cherish the memory of my late father, Major M. Mustafa, my late mother, Mrs. Kulsoom Begum, my late brother, Dr. M. Mukarram, and my late sisters, Mrs. Nasimun Nisa Farhat, Shabnanand, and Razia. Additionally, I am grateful for the support and guidance of my late father-in-law, CMO Dr. M. Shoeb Alam Khan.

My heartfelt thanks extend to all my friends, families, relatives, and teachers who have continuously inspired and provided moral support to me throughout my journey. Special gratitude is owed to Mrs. Nuzhat Alam Akram for her invaluable financial support towards the completion of this book. Last but not least, I express my appreciation to the members of my book project team, whose collaboration and assistance were instrumental in bringing this endeavor to fruition.

With sincere appreciation,

Dr. Akram Mohammad, Ph.D. (Chem.), LL.M

About the Author

Dr. Akram Mohammad, Ph.D. (Chem.), LL.M., is the author of the book "Wars, Refugees, Human Rights, and World Peace." Dr. Akram earned his Ph.D. in Chemistry from Aligarh Muslim University, Aligarh, India, his LL.M. from Lucknow University, India, and his M.Sc. in Accelerator Mass Spectrometry  (AMS) from the University of Ottawa, Canada. He also completed diploma courses in Paralegal Studies from ACA, Ottawa, and Regulatory Affairs from AAPS, Toronto.

Dr. Akram conducted his M.Phil. and Ph.D. research at the Central Drug Research Institute (CDRI), Lucknow, and served as a Research Associate at the Industrial Toxicology Research Centre (ITRC), Lucknow, India. He received fellowships from the Council of Scientific and Industrial Research (CSIR) and the Indian Council of Medical Research (ICMR), Delhi. Additionally, he held the position of president at the Research Scientist and Fellow Association (RSFA) in Lucknow, India. His LL.M. thesis focused on "Crime against Women." In his career, Dr. Akram has held various positions, including Scientist at the Food and Agriculture Organization (FAO) of the United Nations in Riyadh, Saudi Arabia, and Professor and Chairman of the Examination Board at the College of Pharmacy, Qassim University, Saudi Arabia. He also worked as a Scientific Researcher at Health Canada, Ottawa, where he discovered and developed the Flow-through Diffusion Cell, a device used to measure toxic chemicals in human skin. Furthermore, he served as a Research and Teaching Associate at Carleton University, the National Research Council (NRC), and the University of Ottawa, Canada.

Dr. Akram was born in the Army Hospital, Madras, T.N., India, and spent his childhood in his paternal grandparents' home in Jamuwawu, Bilthraroad, Ballia, UP, and his maternal grandparents' home in Khairaty, Sivan-Chapra, Bihar, India. He currently resides with his family in Nepean, Ottawa, Ontario, Canada. His education journey took him through various cities in India and Canada, including Jamuwawu, Ballia; Jabalpur, M.P.; Allahabad, U.P.; Aligarh Muslim University, Aligarh; and Lucknow University.

Dr. Akram's late father, Major M. Mustafa, was an Indian Army Officer, and his late mother, Mrs. Kulsoom Begum, was a homemaker. He has four brothers: Col. Dr. Azam, Dr. Muazzam, late Dr. Mukarram, and Prof. Aslam, as well as late sisters Mrs. Nasimun Nisa Farhat, late Miss. Shabnam Mustafa, and late Miss Razia Mustafa.

He married Nuzhat Alam, the daughter of CMO Dr. M. Shoeb Alam and Mrs. Najma Khatoon from Baheri, Ballia, India, in Azamgarh. Dr. Akram and Nuzhat have three daughters: Afreenish, Parihan, and Afrah, and four sons: Azfar, Yawar, Zafar, and Uzair. Their current residence is at 347 Bakewell Crescent, Barrhaven, Nepean, Ottawa, K2G 7E9, Ontario, Canada.

Dr. Akram can be contacted via email at mnakram100@gmail.com.

Preface

In the annals of human history, war has been an ever-present specter, haunting civilizations since the dawn of time. From the primal conflicts of the Stone Age to the devastating modern-day weaponry of atomic, biological, and chemical warfare, the narrative of human existence is fraught with the scars of conflict. It's a narrative that we, as a species, cannot afford to ignore.

As I embark on this journey, delving into the depths of war, refugees, human rights, and the pursuit of world peace, I am compelled by a profound sense of duty to shed light on the plight of the innocent. For too long, the voices of those caught in the crossfire have been silenced, their rights trampled upon amidst the chaos of conflict.

The genesis of this book lies in a deep-seated conviction that every individual, regardless of circumstance, deserves to be treated with dignity and respect. It is an outcry against the senseless violence that tears apart families, communities, and nations, leaving in its wake a trail of suffering and despair.

Through these pages, I aim to trace the evolution of war and its impact on human society, from the earliest skirmishes to the complex geopolitical landscapes of today. But this is not merely a historical account; it is a call to action. It is a plea for compassion, understanding, and, above all, a commitment to upholding the rights of every individual, particularly those displaced by conflict.

The refugee crisis, born out of the ashes of war, is a stark reminder of our collective failure to protect the most vulnerable among us. Yet, despite the darkness, there is hope. With its mandate to safeguard human rights, the United Nations offers a beacon of light in an otherwise tumultuous world. By granting refugees legal recognition and the right to a better future, we can pave the way toward a more peaceful and inclusive society.

As I embark on this exploration of war, refugees, and human rights, I invite you, the reader, to join me in this journey of discovery and reflection. Together, let us raise our voices for peace, justice, and the fundamental rights of all humanity.

Contents

Chapter 1: Introduction

In a world plagued by the echoes of war, where the cries of innocent souls resonate through the corridors of time, I find myself compelled to pen down tales of anguish and resilience. This book, my humble attempt at showcasing empathy, stands as a testament to the great violation of human rights that has unfolded during and after the storms of conflict.

As I gaze upon the pages of history, the ink stains are not merely marks on paper, but reflections of the blood spilled on battlefields and the tears shed in the aftermath. It is a chronicle of humanity's struggle for survival, not only in the face of physical harm but against the erosion of the very essence of what makes us human – our rights.

In the hushed whispers of survivors and the solemn silence of forgotten graves, I find the inspiration to raise a voice that echoes through the annals of time. It is a call to action, a plea for a world where human rights are not merely a buzzword but the cornerstone of our existence. We must transcend the basic provisions of food and water; we must aspire for a society that nurtures the dignity of every individual.

The quest for human rights is not a lofty ideal but a basic tenet that defines our shared humanity. As I embark on this literary journey, I am acutely aware of the responsibility that rests on my shoulders – to shed light on the shadows that linger in the corners of our collective conscience.

The horrors of war leave scars that transcend generations, marking the descendants of the fallen with an indelible ink. It is not enough to provide assistance in the form of rations and relief; we must strive for a world where the rights of the survivors are upheld with the same vigor as the flags that flutter in the winds of peace.

In the pursuit of this noble cause, I am reminded of the words of Eleanor Roosevelt, who declared, "Where, after all, do universal human rights begin? In small places, close to home — so close and so small that they cannot be seen on any maps of the world." It is in these small places, the forgotten corners of our globe, that the battle for human rights is waged daily.

Consider the tale of Aisha, a survivor of a conflict that razed her village to the ground. In the rubble, she clung to the remnants of her shattered life, a mere whisper of the dreams she once held. Aisha's story mirrors the harsh realities faced by countless individuals whose rights are trampled upon in the wake of war.

In the Syrian conflict, which began in 2011, numerous individuals like Aisha experienced the devastation of war. Cities were reduced to ruins, and communities were torn apart. Families were displaced, and their homes turned into battlegrounds. During this chaos, real-life survivors emerged, embodying the indomitable strength of the human spirit.

One such survivor is Malala Yousafzai, a Pakistani education activist. Malala faced the brutal consequences of conflict when, in 2012, she was shot by the Taliban for advocating girls' education in Pakistan's Swat Valley. Miraculously surviving the attack, Malala became a global symbol of resilience and an advocate for the right to education, especially for girls in conflict zones.

Through the eyes of Aisha and the experiences of survivors like Malala, we witness not only the immense challenges wrought by war but also the unwavering courage that propels individuals to rebuild their lives. Aisha's journey becomes a poignant reminder of the broader, real-world implications of armed conflicts on innocent lives.

In the face of such adversity, it is crucial to acknowledge that these survivors' struggles often go unnoticed or underreported. The aftermath of war leaves scars that extend beyond the physical landscape, affecting the mental and emotional well-being of those who survive. Without a concerted effort to shine a light on these stories, the plight of individuals like Aisha risks being overshadowed by the larger geopolitical narrative.

Real-life facts underscore the urgency of addressing the consequences of war on civilian populations. According to the United Nations High Commissioner for Refugees (UNHCR), as of 2021, there were over 80 million forcibly displaced people worldwide, with nearly 26.4 million classified as refugees. These numbers represent not just statistics but human lives disrupted by conflict, seeking refuge and stability.

This book is an anthem for those whose voices are stifled by the cacophony of destruction. It resonates with the echoes of those who dream of a world where the clamor of gunfire is replaced by the harmonious chords of peace. It beckons us to reflect on the words of Martin Luther King Jr., who declared, "Injustice anywhere is a threat to justice everywhere."

The violation of human rights is not confined to the theaters of war; it seeps into the very fabric of our societies. It manifests in the discriminatory policies that marginalize certain communities, in the prejudiced institutions that perpetuate inequality, and in the indifference that allows these injustices to persist. This book is a call to dismantle these barriers and construct a society where the rights of every individual are not contingent on their race, religion, or socio-economic status.

In the pursuit of a just and equitable world, we must confront the uncomfortable truths that fester in the shadows. The stories within these pages serve as a mirror, reflecting the imperfections of our collective humanity. Only by acknowledging these flaws can we begin the transformative journey toward a society where human rights are not a privilege but an inalienable right.

As I pen down these words, I am acutely aware of the power that lies in storytelling. It is through narratives that we bridge the gap between the abstract concept of human rights and the lived experiences of individuals. In the words of Chimamanda Ngozi Adichie, "Stories matter. Many stories matter. Stories have been used to dispossess and to malign, but stories can also be used to empower and to humanize."

This book, then, is a collection of stories that humanize the struggle for rights. It is an exploration of the resilience of the human spirit, an ode to those who, against all odds, continue to stand tall in the face of adversity. Through the narratives woven within these pages, I hope to ignite a spark of empathy that transcends borders and inspires collective action.

In the pursuit of world peace and the ideal human society, we must recognize that the journey is fraught with challenges. It requires dismantling the structures that perpetuate injustice, amplifying the voices of the marginalized, and fostering a global consciousness that values human rights above all else.

Let this book be a clarion call, not just to the intellectuals and policymakers but to every individual who turns these pages. In the words of Mahatma Gandhi, "You must be the change you want to see in the world." The change begins with acknowledging the stories within these pages, understanding the pain and resilience encapsulated in each word, and then channeling that understanding into tangible action.

As we navigate the pages of this narrative, let us reflect on our shared responsibility to be custodians of human rights. Let the stories within these chapters serve as a catalyst for conversations that transcend the barriers of geography, culture, and creed. In the tapestry of our shared humanity, may this book be a thread that binds us together, reminding us that the pursuit of human rights is not just a noble ideal but a collective imperative.

In the realm of human history, the specter of war has haunted our existence since time immemorial. It is a dark chapter that unfolds repeatedly, where people, driven by unknown motives, engage in acts of violence that shatter the very fabric of society. From the annals of ancient conflicts to the present-day horrors of atomic, biological, and even media wars, humanity has witnessed a relentless cycle of destruction.

The recent COVID-19 pandemic has added a new layer to the complexities of our global landscape. In the face of this unseen enemy, the fragility of our interconnected world became painfully evident. The ravages of war, whether conventional or invisible like the pandemic, leave in their wake a trail of refugees

– individuals displaced from their homes, robbed of their sense of belonging.

As I reflect on these profound issues, my gaze is fixed on the plight of those caught in the crossfire of conflicts. Innocent lives, torn apart by forces beyond their control, bear witness to the harsh realities of war. The refugee crisis emerges as a stark consequence, echoing the cries of those who have lost not only their homes but also their human rights.

In the harsh crucible of war, refugees find themselves living in conditions akin to animals, struggling for the most basic necessities like food and shelter. The violation of their rights, a glaring injustice, paints a grim picture of the aftermath of conflict. This is where my journey as a writer begins – with a deep-seated need to amplify the voices of those silenced by the cacophony of war.

The United Nations, with its mission to uphold the dignity and rights of every individual, plays a pivotal role in this narrative. Granting legal rights and U.N. citizenship to refugees signifies a glimmer of hope in an otherwise bleak scenario. This not only provides immediate relief but also opens doors for the future generation to move freely across borders, seeking education and securing their rightful place in the world.

The crux of my book lies in the conviction that advocating for human rights should extend beyond the basic necessities of life. While food and water are essential, the broader spectrum of human rights encompasses the right to live without fear, the right to education, and the right to a future unmarred by the shadows of war. World peace, a lofty ideal, becomes achievable when we address the root causes of conflict and advocate for the rights of the most vulnerable.

My decision to embark on this literary journey is rooted in the belief that words have the power to transcend boundaries and evoke empathy. By narrating the stories of those affected by war and championing the cause of human rights, I hope to contribute to a collective awakening. It is not just about documenting the horrors of war but about inspiring change, fostering understanding, and sowing the seeds of compassion.

As a writer, I bring my own background into the narrative. Having witnessed the struggles of the displaced and the disenfranchised, I carry with me a sense of responsibility to give voice to the voiceless. It is not merely an academic pursuit but a deeply personal quest to make a difference in the world, one written word at a time.

From the ancient battlefields to the present era of atomic, biological, chemical, and media wars, the specter of conflict has cast a long and ominous shadow over our collective existence. The toll of war is immeasurable, marked by the loss of innocent lives and the shattering of societies.

One cannot help but ponder the senselessness of it all — why do people engage in acts of violence, tearing apart the very fabric of human civilization? The echoes of ancient wars still reverberate in the corridors of time, reminding us that the propensity for conflict is deeply ingrained in our species. However, the modern era has brought forth new and terrifying forms of warfare, pushing humanity to the brink of self-destruction.

The advent of atomic warfare, with its devastating power, has raised the stakes to unimaginable heights. The fear of annihilation looms large, casting a pall over international relations and diplomacy. Biological warfare, as exemplified by the COVID-19 pandemic, underscores the interconnectedness of our world – a single microscopic entity can bring nations to their knees, transcending borders and ideologies.

Chemical warfare adds another layer of horror to conflicts as unseen agents unleash suffering and death. The scars left by such weapons persist, both in the physical landscapes and the collective psyche of affected communities. In the digital age, the battleground has expanded to include the world of information – media wars manipulate narratives, sow discord, and erode the foundations of trust.

As the flames of war rage on, one of its most tragic consequences is the plight of refugees. Forced to flee their homes due to conflict, these individuals find themselves in a stateless limbo, their lives upended and their human rights trampled upon. The refugee crisis is a stark reminder of the human cost of war – families torn apart, dreams shattered, and the basic right to a dignified life stripped away.

Living in makeshift camps, refugees endure conditions akin to those of animals, struggling for the most basic necessities, such as food and shelter. The echoes of their suffering reverberate across the international community, demanding a response that goes beyond borders and politics. The United Nations, recognizing the urgency of the situation, has taken steps to provide legal protection and a semblance of identity to refugees through UN citizenship.

Granting refugees a legal status not only safeguards their human rights but also opens doors to a brighter future for their children. UN citizenship allows refugee children to access education and opportunities that transcend the confines of displacement. It is a beacon of hope in the darkness of uncertainty, a testament to the idea that every individual, regardless of their circumstances, deserves a chance at a meaningful life.

In embracing the principles of UN citizenship for refugees, we pave the way for a more interconnected and compassionate world. The education of refugee children becomes an investment in the future, a countermeasure against the perpetuation of cycles of violence and displacement. By providing them with the tools to build a better future, we contribute to the long-term goal of fostering global peace.

As we journey through the pages of this exploration into the intertwined themes of war, refugees, human rights, and world peace, the narrative unfolds like a poignant tapestry. It is a narrative that beckons us to reflect on the past, confront the harsh realities of the present, and envision a future where the ravages of war are replaced by the promise of peace.

By the end of this book, you will not only have gained insights into the historical and contemporary dimensions of war but will also have explored the profound impact of conflict on the lives of refugees. The struggles and resilience of individuals caught in the crossfire will serve as a poignant reminder of our shared humanity.

Through the lens of UN citizenship, readers will witness the transformative power of providing legal status to refugees, offering them a lifeline out of the abyss of statelessness. The stories of those who have risen above the challenges of displacement will inspire hope and reaffirm the belief that, even in the face of seemingly insurmountable odds, humanity has the capacity for compassion, empathy, and positive change.

As we navigate the complexities of war and its aftermath, the overarching message of this book is clear: In addressing the root causes of conflict, championing the rights of refugees, and embracing the principles of global citizenship, we can collectively work toward a world where the flames of war are extinguished, and the seeds of peace are sown for generations to come.

Chapter 2: War

War has been a constant companion of humanity throughout its history. The story of our species is marked by conflicts, battles, and wars that have shaped the course of civilizations. The reasons for war are diverse and complex, ranging from territorial disputes and resource competition to ideological differences and struggles for power. Despite the devastating consequences that wars bring, they remain a common occurrence in human society.

In the annals of history, countless wars have left their indelible marks on the world. One such conflict that continues to capture the world's attention is the Israeli-Palestinian conflict, particularly the ongoing struggles in Gaza. The Gaza Strip, a small piece of land on the eastern coast of the Mediterranean Sea, has been a hotbed of tension and violence for decades. The root causes of the conflict are deeply rooted in historical, religious, and political factors, making it a poignant example of the complexities that often lead to war.

One such case is the Gaza conflict involving the State of Israel and the Palestinian territories, primarily the Gaza Strip, governed by the Palestinian political and militant group Hamas. The underlying issues include disputes over land, historical grievances, and the broader Arab-Israeli conflict. The conflict has resulted in numerous armed conflicts, with both sides experiencing immense human suffering and loss. The civilian population, including women and children, often bears the brunt of the violence, highlighting the tragic and indiscriminate nature of war.

Quotes from those directly affected by the conflict provide a stark reminder of the human toll. A Gazan resident who has experienced the harsh realities of war once said, "In war, there are no winners, only losers. We lose our homes, our loved ones, and our sense of security. The scars of war run deep, leaving wounds that may never fully heal."

The Gaza conflict is just one example of the pervasive nature of war in our world. Throughout history, nations and communities have engaged in conflicts for various reasons, leaving behind a trail of destruction and loss. The human cost of war is immeasurable, as lives are lost, families torn apart, and entire communities upended. The toll extends beyond the physical battlefield to the psychological and emotional realms, affecting generations long after the guns fall silent.

War, in its essence, represents a failure of diplomacy and conflict resolution. As nations and groups resort to armed confrontations, it reflects an inability to find peaceful solutions to disputes. The reasons for going to war are diverse, but the common thread often involves a breakdown in communication, a lack of understanding, and an unwillingness to compromise.

The historical record is replete with examples of wars fought over territorial expansion. Empires rose and fell as nations sought to secure more land and resources. The conquests of Alexander the Great, the Roman Empire, and the expansionist ambitions of various European powers are testaments to the role territorial disputes have played in shaping the world.

In more recent times, the invasion of Iraq in 2003 serves as a sobering example of the consequences of geopolitical power struggles. The justifications for the war were complex and multifaceted, involving claims of weapons of mass destruction, regime change, and the broader War on Terror. The aftermath revealed the intricate challenges of nation-building and the unforeseen consequences of military interventions.

War is not confined to nation-states alone; internal conflicts, often characterized by civil wars, insurgency, and rebellion, are equally prevalent. The Syrian Civil War, which erupted in 2011, stands as a tragic illustration of internal strife leading to widespread destruction and displacement. The complex web of political, ethnic, and religious factors involved has made the conflict exceptionally challenging to resolve, leaving millions of Syrians caught in the crossfire.

In the words of a Syrian refugee, "War is like a tornado that sweeps away everything in its path. We lose our homes, our friends, and our sense of normalcy. The scars of war stay with us, haunting our dreams and shaping our futures."

Ideological differences have also fueled many conflicts throughout history. The Cold War, a protracted period of geopolitical tension between the United States and the Soviet Union, exemplifies how ideological rivalries can bring the world to the brink of war. The arms race, proxy wars, and the constant threat of nuclear annihilation hung heavily over the global psyche for decades.

While the Cold War never escalated into a direct military confrontation between the superpowers, its influence was felt in various regional conflicts. The Korean War and the Vietnam War, both proxy battles between the United States and the Soviet

Union, left indelible marks on the affected nations and their populations. The human cost of these conflicts was staggering, with millions of lives lost and societies torn apart.

In the contemporary landscape, the specter of war looms in various forms. Cyber warfare, economic sanctions, and diplomatic tensions underscore the diverse ways in which nations engage in conflicts without resorting to traditional military means. The interconnected nature of the global community means that the consequences of these conflicts can reverberate far beyond the borders of the involved nations.

The prevalence of war in human history prompts reflection on the nature of our species. While humans can profoundly act with compassion, creativity, and cooperation, the propensity for conflict is an undeniable aspect of our collective existence. Understanding the root causes of war is essential for fostering a more peaceful world.

The quest for peace requires addressing the underlying issues that often lead to conflict. Diplomacy, dialogue, and a commitment to understanding different perspectives are crucial in preventing the escalation of disputes into full-blown wars. International organizations, such as the United Nations, play a pivotal role in facilitating communication and mediating conflicts to prevent them from spiraling out of control.

In the words of former UN Secretary-General Kofi Annan, "More than ever before in human history, we share a common destiny. We can master it only if we face it together. And that, my friends, is why we have the United Nations."

War, however, is not solely a matter for governments and international bodies. Individuals, too, play a crucial role in shaping the world's collective destiny. The choices we make, the values we uphold, and our commitment to empathy and understanding all contribute to the broader tapestry of human interaction.

War remains a common and unfortunate reality in human society. The reasons for conflict are myriad, ranging from territorial disputes and resource competition to ideological differences and struggles for power. Real-life examples, such as the Israeli-Palestinian conflict in Gaza, provide poignant illustrations of the human toll of war. From historical conflicts like the Cold War to contemporary challenges like cyber warfare, the prevalence of conflict underscores the need for a concerted effort to promote peace.

Addressing the root causes of war requires a commitment to diplomacy, dialogue, and understanding. The human capacity for compassion and cooperation must be harnessed to create a world where conflicts are resolved through peaceful means. As we navigate the complexities of our shared destiny, the lessons of history and the voices of those directly affected by war serve as reminders of the urgent need for a more peaceful and harmonious world.

War, with its destructive force and chaotic nature, invariably leads to the tragic loss of innocent lives. The toll on civilians, often caught in the crossfire, is a stark and heart-wrenching reality that accompanies armed conflicts. The death of innocent people is an undeniable consequence of war, and understanding this aspect sheds light on the profound human cost of armed hostilities.

In the middle of conflict, civilians find themselves in the unenviable position of being non-combatants, yet they bear the brunt of the violence. The impact on vulnerable populations, including women, children, and the elderly, is particularly severe. The destruction of homes, displacement, and the disruption of essential services create a dire humanitarian crisis, exacerbating the suffering of those who have no direct involvement in the hostilities.

The wars in Syria and Yemen offer distressing contemporary examples of how innocent lives become casualties of armed conflicts. In Syria, the protracted civil war has resulted in the deaths of hundreds of thousands of civilians. The indiscriminate targeting of populated areas, including schools and hospitals, has led to a staggering loss of innocent lives. The haunting images of children pulled from the rubble of bombed buildings serve as a poignant reminder of the vulnerability of those who have no role in the political and military decisions that precipitate conflict.

In Yemen, a nation grappling with internal strife and external interventions, the toll on civilians is equally devastating. The conflict has given rise to a humanitarian crisis, with millions facing food insecurity and the collapse of essential services. The targeting of civilian infrastructure, such as markets and hospitals, has resulted in countless innocent lives lost. The international community has witnessed the unfolding tragedy, yet finding a resolution to the conflict remains a complex challenge.

Quotes from those directly affected by such conflicts provide a glimpse into the human suffering. A survivor of the Syrian conflict expressed, "War stole my childhood and my dreams. I lost my family, my friends, and everything I knew. The sound of explosions is etched in my memory, a constant reminder of the price innocent people pay for the decisions of others."

The death of innocent people in war is not confined to distant conflicts; it reverberates across the globe, fostering empathy and a shared responsibility to prevent such tragedies. The international community often grapples with the ethical dimensions of armed interventions, weighing the imperative to protect civilians against the potential risks and unintended consequences of military actions.

The concept of a "just war" has been debated throughout history, emphasizing the need for ethical considerations in the conduct of armed conflicts. However, the reality often falls short of these ideals, as the fog of war obscures distinctions between combatants and non-combatants. Modern warfare, with its advanced weaponry and tactics, has made it increasingly challenging to minimize civilian casualties.

The tragic events of war transcend geopolitical boundaries, prompting reflections on the collective responsibility to prevent and mitigate the impact on innocent lives. The words of Eleanor Roosevelt, a champion of human rights, resonate: "Where, after all, do universal human rights begin? In small places, close to home—so close and so small that they cannot be seen on any map of the world. Unless these rights have meaning there, they have little meaning anywhere."

In the age of information, the world witnesses the consequences of war in real-time. The power of social media and instant communication brings the human stories of conflict to the forefront, making it impossible to turn a blind eye to the suffering of innocent people. The global community is confronted with the stark choice of either standing idly by or actively working toward preventing further loss of life.

Moreover, the death of innocent people in war raises fundamental questions about the effectiveness of military interventions and the pursuit of alternative, diplomatic solutions. The long-term consequences of conflict extend beyond the immediate loss of lives, shaping the trajectory of nations and communities for generations. Rebuilding shattered societies, healing the psychological wounds of survivors, and addressing the root causes of conflict demands a sustained and comprehensive approach.

In the words of Mahatma Gandhi, "An eye for an eye only ends up making the whole world blind." The cyclical nature of revenge and retaliation perpetuates a cycle of violence that claims the lives of innocent people. Breaking this cycle requires a commitment to dialogue, diplomacy, and the pursuit of justice.

The death of innocent people in war underscores the urgency of fostering a culture of peace and conflict resolution. Education, empathy, and a global commitment to human rights are essential components of a world where armed conflicts are the exception rather than the norm. As we reflect on the profound impact of war on innocent lives, the imperative to work toward a more just and peaceful world becomes all the more evident.

The destructive force of war extends far beyond the physical battlefield, permeating the very fabric of human society. The impact of armed conflicts on communities, institutions, and the social fabric is profound and enduring. War leaves scars that go beyond the immediate loss of life, wreaking havoc on the structures that bind societies together.

One of the most palpable ways in which war destroys human society is through the displacement of populations. The upheaval caused by conflict forces people to flee their homes, abandoning the familiar for the uncertainty of displacement. The Syrian Civil War, for instance, has led to one of the largest refugee crises in recent history, with millions seeking shelter in neighboring countries and beyond. The displacement disrupts social networks, erodes cultural ties, and places immense strain on host communities and nations.

Moreover, the destruction of infrastructure during war exacerbates the challenges faced by societies. Schools, hospitals, and essential services often become casualties of armed conflicts, leaving communities without the foundational elements necessary for social cohesion. The rebuilding process is arduous and prolonged, hindering the restoration of normalcy and impeding the development of future generations.

The toll on education is particularly devastating. Schools, which should be sanctuaries for learning and growth, become battlegrounds or collateral damage in war. Children are robbed of their right to education, perpetuating cycles of poverty and hindering the intellectual and social development of entire generations. The loss of educational opportunities reverberates for years, impacting not only individual lives but also the overall progress of societies.

The psychological impact of war on individuals and communities is another aspect of societal destruction. The trauma experienced by those living in conflict zones, whether due to direct exposure to violence or the loss of loved ones, leaves lasting scars. The mental health toll of war is often underestimated, with post-traumatic stress disorder (PTSD) and other mental health conditions affecting individuals long after the guns fall silent.

Real-life stories from war-torn regions echo the profound psychological toll. A survivor of the Bosnian War, reflecting on the enduring scars of conflict, stated, *"The buildings may be rebuilt, but the memories of war linger in the minds of those who lived through it. The sound of sirens, the smell of smoke – they trigger memories that can never be erased."*

War also erodes the bonds of trust within societies. The breakdown of social cohesion, fueled by fear, suspicion, and often, ethnic or sectarian divisions, creates lasting rifts. Rebuilding trust becomes a monumental task as communities struggle to reconcile with the past and forge a collective identity that transcends the scars of conflict.

In the aftermath of war, the challenge of transitional justice emerges. The need to address past atrocities, hold perpetrators accountable, and provide reparations for victims is crucial for healing and reconciliation. However, the pursuit of justice is often fraught with challenges, as political considerations, power dynamics, and the complexities of post-conflict environments complicate the path to accountability.

The impact of war on human society is not confined to physical or visible destruction. It extends to the erosion of values, the distortion of cultural identity, and the perversion of moral compasses. The desperation bred by conflict sometimes leads to adopting extreme ideologies or tolerating atrocities in the pursuit of perceived survival. The consequences of such shifts in societal norms can linger long after the immediate conflict subsides.

Real-life examples, such as the aftermath of the Rwandan Genocide, illustrate the challenges of rebuilding societies shattered by war. The process of reconciliation and rebuilding trust in the aftermath of such atrocities is slow and requires sustained effort. As societies grapple with the consequences of war, the need for international support and solidarity becomes evident.

The destruction wrought by war on human society is multifaceted and enduring. The displacement of populations, the destruction of infrastructure, the erosion of trust, and the profound psychological toll collectively shape the trajectory of nations and communities long after the cessation of hostilities. As we reflect on the devastating impact of war on human society, the imperative to work toward a world where peaceful resolution of conflicts is prioritized becomes all the more urgent.

Chapter 3: The History of War

In the annals of human history, there exists a chapter that marks the inception of organized conflict, a rudimentary yet pivotal moment that laid the foundation for the wars that would follow in time. This chapter takes us back to a time when civilization was still in its infancy when the concept of conflict resolution was a nascent idea.

Our journey begins in the cradle of civilization, the ancient land of Sumer, around 2700 BCE. Picture a landscape dominated by the Tigris and Euphrates rivers, a fertile plain where the first city-states emerged. In this environment of burgeoning societies, the seeds of conflict were sown.

It all started with the struggle for resources. The river valleys, while providing fertile grounds for agriculture, were limited in space. As populations grew, the demand for arable land increased, sparking tensions between neighboring communities. The quest for survival set the stage for what would become the first recorded war in history.

The city-state of Lagash and the city-state of Umma found themselves at the epicenter of this embryonic conflict. The dispute revolved around a piece of land called Gu'edena, a territory crucial for agricultural prosperity. The leaders of both city-states, ensconced in the practicalities of survival, couldn't find a compromise.

In this era, warfare was a rudimentary affair. No grand strategies or intricate tactics; instead, it was a clash of manpower, a contest of strength and will. The soldiers, equipped with primitive weapons—spears, slings, and simple bronze swords—marched to the battlefield, driven by the imperative to secure their way of life.

The Battle of Gu'edena unfolded with a stark simplicity. The soldiers, clad in basic armor, faced each other across the contested terrain. The clash was not about glory or conquest; it was about sustenance. As the first blows were struck, the echoes of conflict reverberated through history, marking a turning point in the evolution of human societies.

The records of this ancient war are etched in the form of cuneiform inscriptions on clay tablets. These tablets, discovered by modern archaeologists, provide a glimpse into the stark realities of the time. The inscriptions detail the grievances, the mobilization of forces, and the aftermath of the conflict.

The war between Lagash and Umma was not an isolated incident; rather, it was a precursor to a series of conflicts that would shape the course of history. The scarcity of resources, territorial disputes, and the struggle for survival continued to fuel the flames of warfare in the ancient world.

What is remarkable about this chapter in history is the absence of any grand ideological or political motivations behind the conflict. It was not a war of ideals or principles but a battle born out of necessity. In the harsh crucible of early civilization, the primordial instinct to protect one's livelihood took precedence over abstract concepts of glory or honor.

The aftermath of the war was not characterized by victors celebrating their conquest but by pragmatic negotiations. The leaders of Lagash and Umma, realizing the futility of perpetual conflict, engaged in discussions to delineate their respective territories. A boundary stone, known as the Stele of the Vultures, was erected to mark the agreed-upon border. It stands as a tangible symbol of the resolution reached through the crucible of conflict.

As we reflect on this ancient war, it serves as a stark reminder of the fundamental human experience— the struggle for survival. In the absence of advanced diplomatic frameworks or international institutions, early civilizations relied on the crude tool of war to resolve disputes. It was a brutal, unrefined approach, but one that reflected the harsh realities of a world grappling with the challenges of coexistence.

The significance of this first recorded war goes beyond its immediate context. It laid the groundwork for the evolution of conflict resolution mechanisms. As civilizations progressed, so did the sophistication of warfare and, concurrently, the need for more nuanced methods of negotiation and peacekeeping.

In human history, the Battle of Gu'edena stands as a foundation of struggle, survival, and adaptation. It was not a glorious chapter, nor was it a tale of valor sung by bards; instead, it was a pragmatic account of humanity's earliest attempts to navigate the complexities of communal living.

As we turn the pages of this ancient chapter, we must resist the temptation to romanticize or vilify the actors involved. The leaders of Lagash and Umma were not warmongers driven by a thirst for conquest; they were pragmatists grappling with the challenges of resource scarcity. Their decisions, shaped by the harsh realities of their time, set the precedent for the complex dance between conflict and resolution that would unfold in the millennia to come.

The echoes of the Battle of Gu'edena lingered in the ancient air, setting a precedent for the nature of conflicts that would unfold across the pages of history. As civilizations burgeoned and interacted, warfare became an integral aspect of their narratives, shaped by the socio-economic and political landscapes of the time.

In the vast expanse of the ancient world, from the Nile to the Yellow River, conflicts arose for a myriad of reasons. Beyond resource scarcity, as seen in the Sumerian city-states, the motivations for war became more diverse. Territorial expansion, competition for trade routes, and the pursuit of power and prestige emerged as driving forces behind the clashes between ancient societies.

The pharaohs of Egypt, ruling over the fertile banks of the Nile, engaged in military campaigns not only to protect their domains but also to expand their influence. The inscriptions on the walls of temples and tombs depict the grandeur of these military expeditions, showcasing the might of chariots, archers, and foot soldiers.

In the ancient Mediterranean, the city-state of Athens clashed with the Persian Empire during the Greco-Persian Wars. Here, the motivations transcended mere survival; they encompassed notions of freedom, autonomy, and the defense of democratic ideals. The Battle of Marathon, a pivotal engagement in this conflict, unfolded on the basis of ideological differences rather than resource disputes.

In the cradle of ancient China, the warring states period marked an era of intense conflict as regional powers vied for supremacy. The philosophy of Sun Tzu, encapsulated in "The Art of War," became a guide for military strategy, emphasizing the importance of tactics, espionage, and understanding the terrain.

The ancient Indian subcontinent, too, witnessed its share of conflicts. The Mahabharata, an epic poem, not only recounts a mythical war between rival factions but also delves into the complex ethical and moral dilemmas faced by its characters. It provides insights into the multifaceted nature of warfare, where familial bonds, righteousness, and political ambitions intertwine on the battlefield.

As we traverse the ancient landscapes of Mesopotamia, Egypt, Greece, China, and India, a common thread emerges: the ubiquity of warfare as a means of asserting influence, protecting interests, or pursuing grander ambitions. However, it is crucial to avoid the trap of oversimplification. The motivations behind ancient wars were as diverse as the civilizations themselves, shaped by cultural, political, and economic contexts.

The methods of warfare were equally diverse. From the tightly disciplined phalanx formations of Greek hoplites to the chariot charges of the ancient Egyptians, each society developed its unique military traditions. Technological advancements, such as the introduction of iron weapons, revolutionized the nature of conflict, allowing for more lethal and efficient means of waging war.

Yet, for all their differences, the ancient civilizations shared a common struggle: the challenge of reconciling the necessity of war with the desire for peace and stability. The idea of a "just war" emerged, often intertwined with religious or moral principles that sought to legitimize conflicts. Leaders, priests, and philosophers grappled with the ethical dimensions of warfare, attempting to impose limits on the brutality of human conflict.

In the absence of a global order or international institutions, diplomacy in the ancient world often took a backseat to military might. Treaties were fragile, alliances were fluid, and the balance of power was maintained through a delicate dance of shifting allegiances. The concept of a lasting peace seemed elusive as the empires of old rose and fell, each leaving its mark on the canvas of history.

As we reflect on the ancient world's approach to warfare, it becomes apparent that the roots of contemporary geopolitical struggles trace back to these formative epochs. The lessons learned, sometimes at great cost, laid the groundwork for the evolution of military strategy, diplomatic relations, and the enduring tension between the pursuit of power and the quest for stability.

As we traverse the corridors of time, we witness the ever-shifting landscape of warfare, an intricate tapestry woven by the hands of history. From the rudimentary conflicts of ancient city-states to the complex geopolitical struggles of the modern era, the evolution of warfare reflects not only technological advancements but also the changing dynamics of human societies.

The transition from the ancient to the medieval period marked a shift in the nature of warfare. The emergence of feudalism brought forth a decentralized system of governance, where local lords held sway over territories, raising armies to protect their lands. Battles were often characterized by heavily armored knights on horseback, wielding lances and swords. The feudal code of chivalry, with its emphasis on honor and bravery, added a layer of ritual and decorum to medieval warfare.

The invention of gunpowder in the late medieval period revolutionized the battlefield. Firearms, cannons, and artillery altered the dynamics of warfare, diminishing the dominance of traditional knightly cavalry charges. The advent of the musket and the arquebus ushered in an era where infantry could play a more decisive role, leveling the playing field and reshaping the strategies employed in conflicts.

The early modern period witnessed the rise of professional standing armies, marking a departure from the feudal system of relying on local levies. The Thirty Years' War (1618-1648) in Europe stands as a testament to the devastating impact of prolonged conflict on civilian populations. The notion of the state monopoly on violence solidified during this period, laying the groundwork for the modern nation-state and its role in orchestrating warfare.

The Industrial Revolution brought about seismic changes in the nature of war. Technological advancements, such as the rifling of barrels, steam-powered machinery, and the telegraph, transformed the logistics and tactics of armed conflicts. The mass production of weapons and the mechanization of warfare intensified the scale and brutality of battles, culminating in the trench warfare of World War I.

The 20th century witnessed unprecedented advancements in military technology. The advent of tanks, aircraft, and later, nuclear weapons, reshaped the calculus of warfare. World War II showcased the devastating impact of air raids, blitzkrieg tactics, and the strategic bombing of cities. The horrors of the atomic bombings of Hiroshima and Nagasaki underscored the potential for unparalleled destruction in the modern age.

The post-World War II era brought about the Cold War, a period characterized by ideological rivalries and proxy conflicts between the United States and the Soviet Union. The nuclear arms race loomed large, creating a precarious balance between mutually assured destruction and geopolitical maneuvering. The concept of "total war" took on new dimensions as conflicts became intertwined with ideological struggles on a global scale.

The latter half of the 20th century and the beginning of the 21st century witnessed the rise of asymmetric warfare. Guerrilla tactics, insurgencies, and terrorism became prevalent, challenging traditional military doctrines. The advent of cyber warfare added a new dimension to conflicts, where battles were fought not only on physical battlegrounds but also in the digital realm.

In the contemporary era, the nature of war continues to evolve. Hybrid warfare, which combines conventional military tactics with unconventional methods, blurs the lines between war and peace. The role of non-state actors, such as insurgent groups and terrorist organizations, has become increasingly prominent, posing unique challenges for traditional military forces.

As we survey the evolution of warfare through the ages, it becomes evident that technological progress, changes in political structures, and shifts in societal norms have all played pivotal roles in shaping the nature of armed conflicts. What remains constant, however, is the profound impact of war on human lives and the enduring quest to navigate the complexities of international relations while avoiding the catastrophic consequences of unchecked aggression.

One of the defining features of present-day warfare is the prevalence of asymmetric conflicts. Non-state actors, ranging from insurgent groups to terrorist organizations, have become formidable players on the global stage. The wars in Afghanistan, Iraq, and Syria exemplify the challenges posed by irregular warfare, where conventional military forces contend with elusive adversaries employing guerrilla tactics and blending into civilian populations.

Cyber warfare has emerged as a critical dimension of modern conflicts. States and non-state actors alike leverage the power of the digital realm to conduct espionage, disrupt critical infrastructure, and engage in information warfare. The interconnectedness of the globalized world has made nations vulnerable to cyber attacks, blurring the lines between traditional military engagements and covert operations in the virtual sphere.

The rise of hybrid warfare further complicates the contemporary military landscape. This approach combines conventional military tactics with unconventional methods, including political subversion, economic coercion, and disinformation campaigns. The goal is to achieve strategic objectives without necessarily resorting to open warfare, challenging traditional notions of conflict escalation.

The role of technology in present-day warfare cannot be overstated. Advancements in military hardware, including drones, precision-guided munitions, and artificial intelligence, have transformed the battlefield. Unmanned aerial vehicles, in particular, have altered the dynamics of reconnaissance and targeted strikes, providing militaries with unprecedented capabilities while raising ethical questions about the nature of remote warfare.

Globalization has also influenced the nature of conflicts in the present era. Economic interdependence and the interconnectedness of nations create complex webs of alliances and dependencies. Wars, therefore, have repercussions that extend beyond national borders, impacting economies, refugee crises, and international relations. The concept of "soft power" has gained prominence, emphasizing the importance of cultural influence, diplomacy, and economic leverage in shaping global narratives.

The specter of nuclear weapons, a remnant of the Cold War era, continues to cast a long shadow over international relations. While the likelihood of full-scale nuclear warfare has diminished, the possession of nuclear arsenals by multiple nations introduces a precarious balance of deterrence, highlighting the imperative for diplomatic resolutions to prevent catastrophic scenarios.

Humanitarian concerns remain at the forefront of discussions on present-day warfare. Civilian casualties, displacement, and the impact of conflict on vulnerable populations demand international attention. The ethical dimensions of military interventions and the responsibility to protect civilians underscore the need for a nuanced approach to contemporary conflicts.

In international institutions, the United Nations plays a central role in conflict resolution and peacekeeping. However, the effectiveness of these efforts is often constrained by geopolitical rivalries, competing national interests, and the limitations of enforcing global order. The challenges of achieving consensus in the United Nations Security Council reflect the complexities of navigating the diplomatic landscape in the face of conflict.

As we grapple with the complexities of warfare in the present era, it is essential to recognize the interplay of historical legacies, technological innovations, and geopolitical dynamics. The lessons learned from past conflicts serve as a guide for navigating the challenges of the contemporary world, emphasizing the importance of diplomacy, cooperation, and the pursuit of inclusive, sustainable solutions to conflicts.

In examining the complexities of present-day warfare, the situation in Gaza serves as a poignant example, illustrating the multifaceted nature of contemporary conflicts. The Gaza Strip, a small Palestinian territory bordering Israel and Egypt, has been a focal point of longstanding tensions and conflicts in the Middle East.

The conflict in Gaza is characterized by a combination of historical, political, and ideological factors. Rooted in the Israeli-Palestinian conflict, it involves disputes over territory, sovereignty, and the rights of the Palestinian people. The struggle for self-determination and statehood has led to a series of violent confrontations, often resulting in significant humanitarian challenges.

One recurring element in the Gaza conflict is the use of asymmetric warfare. Palestinian groups, such as Hamas, have employed guerrilla tactics, rocket attacks, and asymmetric warfare strategies against the technologically superior Israeli military. The use of tunnels, homemade rockets, and unconventional methods amplifies the challenges faced by traditional military forces in this protracted conflict.

Moreover, the Gaza conflict has a pronounced humanitarian dimension. The densely populated Gaza Strip is home to a large civilian population that often bears the brunt of the violence. Human rights organizations highlight concerns about civilian casualties, displacement, and the impact of hostilities on essential services such as healthcare, education, and infrastructure.

The role of technology, particularly in terms of military capabilities, is evident in the conflict. Israel's Iron Dome missile defense system, designed to intercept and destroy incoming rockets, showcases the impact of technological advancements on the dynamics of warfare. Simultaneously, the use of social media and digital platforms has transformed the information battlefield, influencing global perceptions and narratives surrounding the conflict.

Efforts to address the Gaza conflict and achieve lasting peace have involved international institutions, including the United Nations. Calls for ceasefires, negotiations, and diplomatic resolutions underscore the complexity of finding a comprehensive and sustainable solution. The challenges of navigating the geopolitical landscape, managing conflicting interests, and addressing the grievances of both parties are indicative of the intricate nature of modern conflicts.

The situation in Gaza serves as a stark reminder of the imperative to prioritize humanitarian considerations in the middle of the conflict. As discussions on contemporary warfare unfold, the Gaza example underscores the need for a comprehensive approach that addresses the immediate security concerns and the underlying issues of justice, self-determination, and the well-being of civilian populations caught in the crossfire.

Chapter 4: The War Fronts Today

In the 21st century, the face of warfare has evolved, presenting a complex and multifaceted landscape that demands our attention. Today's conflicts transcend traditional battlefields, passing through the digital realm, economic structures, and social fabrics. This chapter explores the various dimensions of contemporary warfare, shedding light on the challenges we face in navigating this complex web.

One notable aspect of modern warfare is the prevalence of asymmetry. Unlike conventional wars between nation-states, conflicts today often involve non-state actors, insurgencies, and terrorist organizations. These asymmetrical wars create a dynamic where the lines between combatants and civilians blur, making it challenging to distinguish friend from foe. The War on Terror that emerged after the 9/11 attacks exemplifies this shift, with global powers combating elusive and decentralized adversaries.

Simultaneously, the rise of cyber warfare has introduced a new battleground where nations engage in covert operations, espionage, and disruptive attacks. The interconnectedness of the modern world leaves critical infrastructure vulnerable to cyber threats, ranging from ransomware attacks on corporations to state-sponsored hacking of government systems. The digital landscape has become an arena where conflicts unfold silently, with consequences that can be as devastating as traditional warfare.

Economic warfare is another facet of the contemporary conflict. Sanctions, trade wars, and economic pressure have become tools wielded by nations to assert influence and coerce others. These tactics can cripple economies, destabilize governments, and sow discord within societies. The ongoing tensions between major powers often manifest in economic maneuvers, creating a bloodless form of warfare but not without profound consequences for those caught in the crossfire.

The notion of hybrid warfare further complicates the contemporary scenario. Hybrid warfare combines conventional, unconventional, and irregular methods, blurring the boundaries between war and peace. Proxy conflicts, information warfare, and the use of paramilitary forces characterize this approach. Nations now find themselves engaged in battles that extend beyond military might, incorporating diplomatic, economic, and informational strategies.

In the age of social media, information has become a potent weapon. Propaganda, disinformation, and the manipulation of public opinion play pivotal roles in shaping the narrative of conflicts. The ability to control the information flow influences domestic populations and has international repercussions. In conflicts like the Syrian Civil War or the conflict in Ukraine, the battle for hearts and minds is as crucial as the physical confrontations on the ground.

Humanitarian crises often accompany modern wars, exacerbating the challenges faced by affected populations. The deliberate targeting of civilians, displacement, and the destruction of critical infrastructure have become common tactics. The Syrian refugee crisis, stemming from the protracted conflict in the region, is a stark reminder of the human toll of contemporary warfare.

In addition to these complexities, the proliferation of weapons of mass destruction poses an ever-present threat. The fear of nuclear, chemical, or biological warfare looms large, compelling nations to navigate delicate diplomatic channels to prevent the catastrophic consequences that such weapons could unleash. The denuclearization talks with North Korea and the Iranian nuclear deal are examples of global efforts to curb the spread of these destructive capabilities.

In the middle of these challenges, international institutions and alliances play a crucial role in maintaining stability and addressing conflicts. Organizations like the United Nations (UN), North Atlantic Treaty Organization (NATO), and regional alliances serve as forums for diplomatic dialogue and, in some cases, military cooperation. However, the effectiveness of these institutions is often hampered by geopolitical rivalries and the interests of powerful nations.

The landscape of modern wars is not devoid of hope, though. Grassroots movements, peacebuilding initiatives, and diplomatic efforts continue to strive for conflict resolution. Civil society plays a vital role in holding governments accountable and advocating for peaceful solutions. The power of people to bring about change is evident in movements like the Arab Spring and the push for democracy in Hong Kong.

The face of modern warfare is marked by its complexity and diversity. As we navigate this intricate landscape, it is essential to understand the multifaceted nature of contemporary conflicts.

From asymmetrical warfare and cyber threats to economic pressures and hybrid tactics, the challenges we face demand a comprehensive and adaptive approach.

The specter of war has loomed large, casting its ominous shadow over civilizations. As we delve into the realms of conflict, we encounter a chilling array of warfare – each a distinct manifestation of humanity's darkest instincts.

Atomic War:

The specter of atomic war, characterized by the use of nuclear weapons, looms heavily in the modern geopolitical landscape. The destructive power of nuclear arsenals poses a threat to humanity's very existence. The Cold War era saw the United States and the Soviet Union engaged in a tense nuclear standoff, a period where the world teetered on the edge of potential annihilation. Today, concerns about nuclear proliferation persist, with North Korea's nuclear ambitions and the ongoing tensions between nuclear-armed nations demanding global attention. The potential consequences of an atomic war underscore the necessity for disarmament efforts, diplomatic solutions, and international cooperation.

Biological War:

Biological warfare involves the deliberate use of pathogens or toxins to harm or kill people, animals, or plants. While international treaties such as the Biological Weapons Convention aim to prohibit such activities, the threat remains. The COVID-19 pandemic brought the world's attention to the devastating impact of a naturally occurring virus. However, the fear of intentional release or bioterrorism looms large. The potential use of genetically engineered pathogens raises ethical and security concerns, necessitating strict regulations, robust surveillance, and global collaboration to prevent the misuse of biological agents.

Chemical War:

Chemical warfare involves the use of toxic chemicals to harm or incapacitate adversaries. The Chemical Weapons Convention strives to eliminate the production and use of chemical weapons, yet instances of their deployment persist. The Syrian Civil War witnessed the use of chemical weapons, sparking international condemnation. The challenge lies in enforcing global norms against the use of these weapons and holding perpetrators accountable. International cooperation and diplomatic pressure are vital to ensure compliance with chemical weapons treaties and prevent the resurgence of such brutal tactics.

Media War:

In the era of information, the concept of a "media war" has gained prominence. Information is now a powerful tool in shaping narratives, influencing public opinion, and conducting psychological operations. State-sponsored disinformation campaigns, fake news, and propaganda have become common tactics in conflicts. The weaponization of social media platforms amplifies the impact of these strategies, with the potential to sow discord, manipulate elections, and undermine trust in institutions. Countering the effects of a media war requires media literacy, fact-checking mechanisms, and international efforts to expose and counter disinformation campaigns.

Cyber War:

The digital realm has emerged as a new battleground, with cyber warfare encompassing a range of activities from hacking and espionage to disruptive attacks on critical infrastructure. Nation-states engage in cyber operations to gain strategic advantages, steal sensitive information, or disrupt the operations of adversaries. The Stuxnet virus, which targeted Iran's nuclear program, exemplifies the potential of cyber weapons. Defending against cyber threats requires robust cybersecurity measures, international norms, and cooperation to address the evolving challenges posed by the interconnected nature of the digital world.

Economic War:

Economic warfare involves the use of economic instruments to coerce, destabilize, or gain advantages over adversaries. Sanctions, trade wars, and economic pressure have become commonplace tools in international relations. The economic dimensions of modern conflicts, such as the trade tensions between major powers or the imposition of sanctions on rogue states, showcase how economic power can be leveraged as a form of warfare. Navigating economic wars requires careful diplomacy, international cooperation, and mechanisms to mitigate the impact on civilian populations caught in the crossfire.

The various forms of warfare discussed – atomic, biological, chemical, media, cyber, and economic – have profound and far-reaching implications for human life. The impact extends beyond the immediate physical consequences of conflict, seeping into the fabric of societies, economies, and individual well-being. This reflective discussion explores how these different dimensions of warfare affect human life in diverse and interconnected ways.

Loss of Human Lives and Displacement:

In the event of atomic, biological, or chemical warfare, the most immediate and devastating consequence is the loss of human lives. The sheer destructive power of these weapons can result in mass casualties and irreparable damage to communities. The survivors often face long-term health issues, psychological trauma, and the loss of loved ones. Additionally, these forms of warfare can lead to forced displacement on a massive scale, as people flee the contaminated zones or seek safety from the direct impact of the weapons.

Health and Environmental Consequences:

Biological and chemical warfare not only targets human lives but also has severe consequences for the environment and public health. The release of toxins or pathogens can contaminate air, water, and soil, leading to long-term health issues for both present and future generations. The lingering effects of exposure to such agents can result in chronic illnesses, birth defects, and compromised overall well-being, creating a legacy of suffering that extends well beyond the immediate conflict.

Psychological Impact:

The psychological toll of modern warfare, especially in the context of media and cyber warfare, is significant. The constant barrage of information, often manipulated or false, contributes to heightened anxiety, fear, and uncertainty among populations. In times of conflict, individuals may experience stress, trauma, and a sense of helplessness, exacerbated by the omnipresence of social media amplifying the emotional impact of events. The mental health of communities becomes a casualty of the information war, with long-lasting effects on resilience and social cohesion.

Economic Disruption and Poverty:

Economic warfare, through sanctions or trade conflicts, can have dire consequences for the livelihoods of ordinary people. The imposition of economic measures can lead to job losses, inflation, and a decline in living standards. Entire economies can be crippled, pushing vulnerable populations further into poverty. The economic fallout of warfare disrupts not only the financial stability of nations but also the daily lives of individuals who struggle to meet basic needs in the middle of economic turmoil.

Digital Divide and Vulnerability:

Cyber warfare introduces a new dimension to the human experience, creating a digital divide that impacts access to information, communication, and economic opportunities. In conflicts where cyber-attacks are prevalent, individuals and communities may find themselves cut off from vital resources or exposed to privacy breaches. The vulnerability of critical infrastructure, including healthcare and utilities, poses a direct threat to human life, highlighting the interconnectedness of the digital and physical realms.

Manipulation of Societal Values:

Media warfare, with its arsenal of propaganda and disinformation, plays a pivotal role in shaping societal values and beliefs. The manipulation of narratives can lead to division, polarization, and the erosion of trust within communities. Human relationships become casualties as misinformation fuels animosity and distrust among individuals, fostering an environment where cooperation and empathy become increasingly difficult.

The impact of modern warfare on human life is multi-faceted and pervasive. The loss of life, both immediate and long-term, extends beyond physical casualties to encompass mental health, economic stability, and societal well-being. The interconnected nature of these different dimensions of warfare underscores the need for a holistic approach to conflict resolution that prioritizes the preservation of human life, both in the immediate aftermath and in the years that follow. As we reflect on the consequences of modern warfare, it becomes evident that the true cost is borne not only by nations but, more profoundly, by the individuals and communities caught in the crossfire.

Chapter 5: Refugees

In human history, the creation of boundaries has been a pivotal force in shaping societies and nations. While these lines on maps may seem innocuous, their impact often extends far beyond geopolitical borders. One glaring consequence of the establishment of boundaries has been the refugee crisis, a complex web of human suffering intricately woven into the fabric of our world.

Boundaries, drawn with seemingly simple strokes, carry profound implications. As nations emerged and sought to define their territories, they erected walls, both physical and metaphorical, dividing communities that once coexisted harmoniously. These divisions were often arbitrary, slicing through ethnic, religious, and cultural landscapes without regard for the intricate interweaving of lives.

Consider the aftermath of colonialism, where European powers carved up Africa and the Middle East, creating nations that amalgamated diverse groups within artificial borders. The seeds of discord were sown as these lines disregarded tribal affiliations and longstanding regional dynamics. The result: simmering tensions that eventually boiled over, setting the stage for conflicts that would force countless individuals to flee their homes.

The refugee crisis is, in many ways, a domino effect triggered by the tumbling blocks of geopolitical decisions. As borders solidified, power struggles ensued, and communities found themselves caught in the crossfire. The displaced masses, bereft of choice, embarked on journeys of desperation, seeking refuge from the chaos that unfolded within the confines of newly established borders.

The Syrian conflict stands as a stark example of the collateral damage inflicted by boundaries. When the Syrian government faced opposition, a turbulent struggle for power erupted. As factions clashed within the defined limits of the nation, the civilian population bore the brunt of the violence. Families were torn apart, homes reduced to rubble, and entire communities obliterated. Faced with the horrors of war, Syrians fled, crossing borders in search of safety.

However, the pursuit of refuge is not a straightforward path. Boundaries, both physical and bureaucratic, present formidable obstacles for those seeking sanctuary. The plight of refugees is exacerbated by closed borders, stringent immigration policies, and a global reluctance to extend a helping hand. The lines that once promised security now act as barriers, trapping displaced individuals in perpetual uncertainty.

The refugee crisis is not confined to a single region; it ripples across continents. Consider the Rohingya, a Muslim minority group in Myanmar. Driven by persecution and violence, they sought refuge in neighboring countries. However, their passage was impeded by borders that stood as insurmountable barriers. Denied entry, they faced dire conditions in overcrowded camps, testaments to the tragic consequences of political decisions that determine the fates of the displaced.

In Europe, the refugee crisis took center stage as waves of displaced individuals crossed the Mediterranean Sea in perilous journeys. The borders of European nations became flashpoints, revealing a stark divide in attitudes toward those seeking asylum. While some countries extended a helping hand, others erected walls, both physical and legal, shutting their doors to those desperately seeking safety.

The creation of boundaries has not only fueled conflict and displaced populations but has also given rise to xenophobia and anti-immigrant sentiments. In the face of an influx of refugees, fear of the unknown and economic concerns intertwine, fostering hostility toward those who have been forced to flee their homes. The very lines that were meant to demarcate nations now serve as divisive tools, reinforcing an 'us versus them' mentality.

As we delve deeper into the refugee crisis, a glaring truth emerges: wars are the chief architects of this unfolding human tragedy. Wars, fueled by political strife, territorial disputes, and conflicting ideologies, unleash a relentless wave of displacement, tearing apart the lives of millions who find themselves caught in the crossfire.

One cannot discuss the refugee crisis without acknowledging the profound impact of armed conflicts. Wars, both large-scale and regional, have become breeding grounds for the displacement of entire populations. The consequences of these conflicts ripple far beyond the battlegrounds, extending to neighboring regions and sometimes spanning continents.

Consider the Middle East, a region marred by a complex web of conflicts. The Syrian civil war, ignited by political unrest and exacerbated by external influences, stands as a stark testament to the catastrophic aftermath of armed confrontations. As the war escalated, Syrians witnessed the disintegration of their homes, the loss of loved ones, and the erosion of the very fabric of their society. Faced with such devastation, the only recourse for many was to abandon their homes and embark on perilous journeys in search of safety.

Afghanistan, another war-torn nation, has been a continuous source of displaced individuals. Decades of conflict, marked by foreign invasions, internal power struggles, and the rise of extremist ideologies, have left countless Afghans with no choice but to flee. The consequences of war extend far beyond the immediate violence, as the very infrastructure that sustains communities crumbles under the weight of prolonged conflict.

The impact of wars on the refugee crisis is not confined to the Middle East. Africa has witnessed a multitude of conflicts, from the Rwandan genocide to the ongoing crises in South Sudan and the Democratic Republic of Congo. In each case, the destructive force of war has propelled people to abandon their homes, seek refuge in neighboring countries, or undertake arduous journeys across continents.

The consequences of war-induced displacement are exacerbated by the intricacies of international politics. The refugee crisis often spills across borders, creating complex challenges for nations unprepared to handle an influx of displaced individuals. As geopolitical interests take precedence, the humanitarian needs of refugees are relegated to the background, perpetuating a cycle of suffering.

The plight of refugees is further compounded by the reluctance of nations to provide sanctuary. Strict immigration policies, closed borders, and the rise of anti-refugee sentiments contribute to a global atmosphere where those fleeing conflict are met with hostility rather than compassion. The very nations that may have played a role in the geopolitical landscape leading to these conflicts often turn a blind eye to the human fallout of their actions.

As we navigate the labyrinth of the refugee crisis, a disturbing reality surfaces: amid wars, refugees often find themselves not only displaced from their homes but also stripped of the very rights that define their humanity. The chaos of conflict creates an environment where basic human rights become elusive, and those forced to flee become vulnerable to a myriad of injustices.

The journey of a refugee born out of the crucible of war is fraught with challenges that extend beyond the physical displacement from their homeland. Human rights, the fundamental principles that should safeguard the dignity and well-being of every individual, often crumble in the face of armed conflict.

One glaring violation of human rights occurs in the realm of personal security. Refugees escaping war zones are exposed to unimaginable dangers. Women and children, in particular, become susceptible to exploitation, violence, and trafficking. The very act of fleeing, meant to secure safety, exposes them to a new set of threats that erode their right to live free from harm.

The right to education, a cornerstone of personal development, is another casualty of war for refugees. Displaced children often find themselves without access to schools, their futures held hostage by conflict. The intellectual growth and potential contributions of an entire generation are stunted, perpetuating cycles of poverty and deprivation.

Access to adequate healthcare is a luxury that many refugees are denied. War-torn regions often lack the infrastructure to provide even basic medical services, leaving displaced individuals vulnerable to disease and untreated injuries. The erosion of the right to health not only threatens the well-being of refugees but also poses a global public health risk, as communicable diseases can thrive in overcrowded and unsanitary conditions.

Beyond physical well-being, the mental health of refugees is often neglected, amplifying the erosion of their rights. The trauma of war, the loss of family members, and the uncertainty of their future leave lasting scars. Yet, mental health support is frequently overlooked, leaving refugees to grapple with the invisible wounds of conflict without adequate resources for healing.

The right to work, a crucial aspect of personal autonomy and dignity, is another casualty for refugees. Forced to flee their homes, many find themselves in host countries where employment opportunities are scarce, and legal restrictions often prevent them from contributing meaningfully to society. This economic disenfranchisement perpetuates cycles of poverty and dependency.

Living without life, a paradoxical fate that befalls many refugees, extends beyond the tangible deprivations. The erosion of human rights transforms their existence into a state of limbo, where the struggle for survival overshadows the pursuit of a meaningful and fulfilling life. The promise of a better future, inherent in the concept of seeking refuge, remains elusive as the very rights meant to protect that journey are trampled upon.

In the harsh landscapes of displacement, where the tendrils of conflict have uprooted lives, refugees often find themselves reduced to a primal struggle for survival. In the quest for the most basic human need — sustenance — many are compelled to live in conditions that resemble an animalistic existence, where the pursuit of food becomes a daily battle against desperation.

The refugee experience is deeply entwined with the struggle for nourishment, a fundamental right that becomes a luxury in the wake of war. The displacement caused by conflict often thrusts individuals into unfamiliar territories where food resources are scarce, and the means to acquire them are limited. In this dire reality, refugees find themselves living on the edge, resorting to survival instincts that echo the struggles of the animal kingdom.

Overcrowded refugee camps, hastily erected in the aftermath of conflict, become microcosms of this struggle. Families, once accustomed to the comforts of home, now inhabit makeshift shelters where the lines between human and animal existence blur. The quest for food in these crowded, chaotic spaces becomes a daily ordeal reminiscent of the survival tactics seen in the natural world.

In the absence of proper infrastructure and resources, refugees often resort to foraging for sustenance. Like animals scrounging for scraps, they comb through discarded waste, seeking edible remnants to stave off hunger. This degrading practice not only undermines their dignity but also exposes them to health risks as the search for food becomes intertwined with the filth of their surroundings.

The scarcity of resources also prompts refugees to adopt survival strategies akin to those of wildlife. In some instances, families are forced to rely on the generosity of humanitarian aid, which arrives sporadically and often falls short of meeting the needs of the growing displaced population. The competition for these resources mirrors the territorial struggles observed in the animal kingdom as refugees jostle for their share of a meager bounty.

The search for sustenance extends beyond the confines of refugee camps. Those who venture beyond the safety of these makeshift havens often face perilous journeys in search of food. The very act of securing nourishment becomes a dangerous expedition as refugees navigate unfamiliar terrain, facing the risk of exploitation, violence, and the challenges posed by hostile environments.

In urban settings, where refugees attempt to rebuild their lives, the struggle for food continues. Barriers such as language, legal restrictions, and discrimination often limit their access to employment opportunities, exacerbating the challenges of securing a stable source of nourishment. Faced with these barriers, refugees find themselves grappling with the harsh realities of living on the margins of society, where the pursuit of food becomes a constant battle against the odds.

The animalistic existence forced upon refugees in the pursuit of sustenance is not a choice but a consequence of circumstances beyond their control. It is a stark reminder of the inhumane conditions that emerge when conflicts displace entire populations, leaving them teetering on the brink of survival. As we confront the harsh realities of this existence, it becomes imperative to address not only the immediate need for food but also the systemic issues that perpetuate this cycle of desperation. Only through comprehensive and compassionate interventions can we hope to lift refugees from the shadows of an animalistic struggle and restore their right to live with dignity and humanity.

Chapter 6: Why Should You Care?

In a world grappling with complex issues, the refugee crisis stands as a stark reminder of our shared humanity and the moral responsibility we bear as global citizens. It's not merely a distant problem confined to geopolitical arenas; it's a matter that demands our attention and consideration, not out of obligation, but out of empathy and a recognition of the interconnectedness of our lives.

Firstly, the refugee crisis highlights the harsh realities faced by millions of people around the globe. Imagine being abruptly uprooted from your home, leaving behind familiar faces, places, and a sense of security. This is the daily struggle for refugees – individuals forced to flee their countries due to conflict, persecution, or other life-threatening circumstances. Acknowledging this stark truth should naturally evoke a sense of compassion within us.

These displaced individuals are not faceless statistics; they are human beings with dreams, aspirations, and stories that resonate with the core of our shared experiences. A refugee could be a teacher, a doctor, a parent, or a child with untapped potential. Their displacement is not a choice but a consequence of circumstances beyond their control. As fellow humans, our empathy should extend beyond borders, recognizing the common thread that binds us all – the pursuit of a life free from fear and hardship.

Moreover, the refugee crisis is not an isolated problem; it has ripple effects that touch every corner of the globe. The interconnected nature of our world means that instability in one region can reverberate across borders, affecting economies, security, and the overall well-being of societies. The rise of conflicts, often linked to the root causes of forced displacement, poses a threat to the global order.

Addressing the refugee crisis is not only a humanitarian imperative but also a matter of self-interest. By alleviating the suffering of those who have been displaced, we contribute to fostering stability and security on a global scale. In doing so, we create an environment where nations can thrive economically, socially, and politically. Ignoring the refugee crisis means turning a blind eye to the potential consequences that may affect us all in the long run.

Furthermore, the refugee crisis challenges our commitment to fundamental human rights. Every person, regardless of their nationality or immigration status, is entitled to certain basic rights – the right to life, liberty, and security. We have collectively endorsed these principles through international agreements and conventions as a global community. Ignoring the plight of refugees undermines the very values we claim to hold dear.

Our response to the refugee crisis is a litmus test for the sincerity of our commitment to human rights. It calls for a practical demonstration of our shared values, urging us to move beyond rhetoric and take concrete actions to ensure the dignity and well-being of those who have been forcibly displaced.

Moreover, the refugee crisis is a barometer of our capacity for empathy and compassion. In a world often divided by political, cultural, and ideological differences, the plight of refugees serves as a unifying factor. It transcends borders and challenges us to see beyond the narrow confines of our own lives. By caring about the refugee crisis, we demonstrate our ability to empathize with the suffering of others and extend a helping hand, irrespective of differences.

The question of why we should care about the refugee crisis is not just a matter of altruism; it is an acknowledgment of our shared humanity and a recognition of the interconnectedness that defines our world. The refugee crisis is a call to action, a reminder that our fates are intertwined, and our response to the suffering of others defines the kind of global community we aspire to be. It is not a distant problem; it is a challenge that demands a collective, pragmatic, and compassionate solution for the well-being of our world and the generations to come.

The enduring nature of the refugee crisis is deeply rooted in the unfortunate reality that wars and conflicts seem to be an enduring facet of human history. While the specific geopolitical landscapes and motivations behind these conflicts may shift, the prospect of armed disputes remains a persistent threat to global stability. This stark truth implies that the refugee crisis is not a fleeting issue but rather a chronic challenge that demands sustained attention and thoughtful solutions.

History attests to the cyclical nature of wars, suggesting that conflicts, whether fueled by political, religious, or socioeconomic factors, are unlikely to vanish completely. The roots of these conflicts often run deep, and the complexities involved in resolving them make the prospect of a conflict-free world seem distant. Consequently, the steady stream of displaced individuals seeking refuge is bound to persist, creating an ongoing humanitarian challenge.

The perpetuation of conflicts is influenced by a myriad of factors, including historical grievances, power struggles, resource disparities, and ideological differences. Addressing these underlying causes requires not only a commitment to diplomacy but also a collective effort to address the root issues that fuel tensions. The complexity of international relations, coupled with the multitude of actors involved in conflicts, makes achieving lasting peace a formidable task.

Furthermore, the contemporary geopolitical landscape is marked by a changing array of challenges that contribute to the continuation of wars. Issues such as climate change, resource scarcity, and political instability amplify existing tensions, creating new flashpoints that can trigger conflicts.

Recognizing the enduring nature of conflicts should prompt a shift in our approach to the refugee crisis. Instead of viewing it solely as a temporary emergency, we must acknowledge it as a chronic condition that necessitates long-term strategies. Humanitarian efforts should extend beyond immediate relief to include sustainable solutions that address the root causes of displacement and foster resilience in affected communities.

While it may be unrealistic to expect an absolute end to all wars, concerted international efforts can mitigate their impact and reduce the number of individuals forced to flee their homes. Diplomacy, conflict prevention, and sustainable development initiatives are essential components of a comprehensive approach to managing the refugee crisis in a world where wars persist.

The nature of conflicts suggests that the refugee crisis is not a transitory challenge but a persistent one. Wars may continue to flare up, and their consequences will manifest in the form of displaced populations seeking safety and stability. Recognizing this enduring reality underscores the importance of adopting comprehensive, long-term solutions that address the root causes of conflicts and contribute to a more stable and secure global environment. While the eradication of wars may remain an elusive goal, proactive and sustained efforts can certainly make a meaningful impact in alleviating the human suffering associated with the refugee crisis.

Considering the refugee crisis as a humanitarian crisis demands a decisive response that prioritizes human welfare over political considerations. Humanitarianism compels us to act with compassion, empathy, and a commitment to alleviating the suffering of those affected by displacement. In making decisions on this issue through a humanitarian lens, several key principles and considerations come to the forefront.

Firstly, a humanitarian response requires the international community to recognize the urgency of the situation and mobilize resources effectively. Humanitarian aid must be provided promptly and efficiently to address the immediate needs of refugees, including shelter, food, healthcare, and education. Delays and bureaucratic obstacles in delivering aid can exacerbate the already dire conditions faced by displaced populations.

Secondly, decisions in the context of a humanitarian crisis should prioritize the protection of vulnerable groups, including women, children, the elderly, and individuals with specific needs. Adequate measures must be taken to ensure their safety, both within refugee camps and during the often perilous journey of displacement. This entails robust efforts to prevent and respond to gender-based violence, exploitation, and other threats that disproportionately affect these vulnerable segments of the population.

Furthermore, a humanitarian approach demands a commitment to the principle of non-discrimination. Decisions and actions must be guided by an unwavering dedication to treating all individuals, irrespective of their nationality, ethnicity, religion, or any other characteristic, with dignity and respect. Discrimination has no place in the humanitarian response, and efforts should be made to create inclusive and culturally sensitive environments for refugees.

In the face of a humanitarian crisis, decisions should also prioritize the long-term well-being and self-reliance of displaced populations. This involves not only meeting immediate needs but also supporting sustainable solutions that empower refugees to rebuild their lives. Education and vocational training programs can play a crucial role in enhancing the resilience and capacity of displaced individuals to contribute positively to their communities.

Moreover, a humanitarian perspective necessitates cooperation and collaboration among nations and international organizations. Addressing the refugee crisis requires a collective effort transcending political differences and emphasizing a shared commitment to human welfare. Diplomacy should be leveraged to foster collaboration in finding durable solutions, including the peaceful resolution of conflicts and the promotion of stability in regions prone to displacement.

When approached as a humanitarian crisis, decisions on the refugee crisis must be guided by a steadfast commitment to alleviating human suffering and upholding the dignity of every individual affected. The international community's response should be characterized by timely and effective aid delivery, protection of vulnerable groups, non-discrimination, and a focus on long-term solutions. By prioritizing humanitarian principles, we can work toward a world where the impact of displacement is mitigated and the well-being of those affected is at the forefront of decision-making processes.

Resolving the refugee crisis is intrinsically linked to the pursuit of world peace, as the roots of displacement often lie in conflict and instability. Recognizing the importance of achieving global peace becomes imperative when contemplating lasting solutions to the challenges posed by the refugee crisis. Here's a straightforward exploration of why world peace is crucial for resolving the refugee crisis.

Firstly, peace is a fundamental prerequisite for preventing the emergence of new waves of refugees. The majority of displaced individuals are forced to flee their homes due to conflict, violence, or persecution. Therefore, addressing the underlying causes of these crises through diplomatic means and conflict resolution is paramount. We can preemptively mitigate the conditions that lead to mass displacement by fostering peaceful relations among nations and within regions.

Moreover, a world at peace enables the safe and voluntary return of refugees to their countries of origin. Sustainable peace agreements provide a conducive environment for rebuilding shattered communities and infrastructure. When conflicts cease, displaced populations can return home without fear of further harm, contributing to the overall reduction of refugee numbers.

Additionally, world peace is essential for fostering stability and development in regions prone to displacement. Prolonged conflicts not only displace populations but also hinder economic growth, disrupt education, and strain social structures. Achieving and maintaining peace allows communities to rebuild, invest in their future, and create conditions that discourage mass migration.

Furthermore, diplomatic efforts to prevent and resolve conflicts contribute to the protection of human rights. In times of war, civilians often bear the brunt of violence and persecution, leading to forced displacement. By actively pursuing peace, the international community can uphold human rights principles, ensuring that individuals are not subjected to the hardships of displacement in the first place.

The interconnected nature of global affairs means that conflicts in one region can have far-reaching consequences. A lack of world peace not only perpetuates existing refugee crises but can also contribute to the emergence of new ones. It underscores the importance of a collective commitment to conflict prevention, diplomacy, and international cooperation as essential tools for addressing the root causes of displacement.

The resolution of the refugee crisis hinges on the achievement of world peace. Peaceful relations among nations and conflict resolution efforts are ethical imperatives and pragmatic steps toward reducing the prevalence of forced displacement. By prioritizing global peace, we lay the foundation for a world where the refugee crisis is mitigated, and individuals can live safely and in their own communities.

Chapter 7: The UN Solution

The United Nations (UN) has put forth a proposal that aims to address the legal rights of refugees through the establishment of UN citizenship. This proposition emerges as a response to the pressing need for a more comprehensive and standardized framework to safeguard the rights of displaced individuals worldwide.

At its core, the UN's proposal seeks to create a universal legal status for refugees, transcending the limitations of nationality or the lack thereof. This envisioned UN citizenship is not intended to replace existing national citizenship but rather to act as a supplementary legal identity that grants refugees certain fundamental rights and protections.

The rationale behind this proposal stems from the inherent challenges faced by refugees, who often find themselves in precarious situations without a recognized legal status. In the absence of a concrete legal identity, refugees encounter barriers to accessing essential services, including education, healthcare, and employment. The UN envisions that by establishing a uniform legal framework, the plight of refugees can be alleviated, offering them a more stable and secure existence.

One of the primary objectives of the proposed UN citizenship is to ensure that refugees have the right to work in their host countries. Employment is not only a means of economic sustenance but also a pathway to integration and self-reliance. The proposal emphasizes the importance of empowering refugees to contribute positively to their host communities, fostering a sense of dignity and self-worth.

Furthermore, the UN envisions that this new legal status would facilitate refugees' access to education. By providing a recognized legal identity, barriers to enrollment and participation in educational institutions can be dismantled. Education is a fundamental right that not only equips individuals with skills and knowledge but also plays a pivotal role in the long-term development of communities.

The proposal also addresses the critical issue of family reunification. Under the current patchwork of national laws and regulations, many refugees face significant obstacles in reuniting with their family members. The UN's proposition aims to streamline and simplify these processes, recognizing the importance of maintaining family unity in the face of displacement.

While the concept of UN citizenship may seem ambitious, it is rooted in the understanding that traditional national frameworks often fall short of adequately protecting the rights of refugees. The UN seeks to create a more equitable and just system that transcends geopolitical boundaries by providing a standardized legal identity.

Critics argue that such a proposal may face resistance from sovereign nations reluctant to relinquish control over their citizenship policies. However, proponents contend that the current refugee crisis necessitates bold and innovative solutions that go beyond the limitations of traditional approaches.

Additionally, the UN recognizes the need for a robust monitoring and enforcement mechanism to ensure the effective implementation of this proposed UN citizenship. Without a mechanism to hold nations accountable for upholding the rights of refugees, the envisioned benefits may remain elusive.

The UN's proposal for UN citizenship represents a bold step toward addressing the legal rights of refugees on a global scale. By creating a standardized legal identity, the UN aims to dismantle barriers that impede refugees from accessing essential services and opportunities. While challenges and resistance may arise, the urgency of the global refugee crisis underscores the need for innovative and comprehensive solutions that transcend national boundaries. The proposal stands as a testament to the international community's commitment to ensuring the rights and dignity of every individual, regardless of their displacement status.

The proposal for providing UN citizenship to refugee children opens up a discussion on the potential for these young individuals to have the freedom to move globally for the purpose of education and securing their future. This envisioned mobility is seen as a transformative step toward breaking down barriers often hindering displaced children from accessing quality education and pursuing opportunities beyond their immediate surroundings.

The primary objective of granting UN citizenship to refugee children is to afford them the right to move freely across borders for educational purposes. This means that, regardless of their displacement status or the geopolitical context of their host country, these children would have the opportunity to seek education in any part of the world. This freedom of movement is perceived as a powerful tool in overcoming the limitations imposed by conflict or displacement and ensuring that these young minds can access the best educational resources available globally.

Education is considered a fundamental right for every child, irrespective of their circumstances. By providing UN citizenship to refugee children, the international community aims to create a framework where educational opportunities are not restricted by geopolitical boundaries. This approach acknowledges the potential of these young individuals to contribute meaningfully to the global community, armed with knowledge and skills acquired through diverse educational experiences.

The proposal emphasizes the importance of facilitating the seamless integration of refugee children into educational systems worldwide. With UN citizenship, these children would be able to enroll in schools, colleges, and universities without facing the bureaucratic hurdles that often accompany displacement. This ease of access is envisioned to empower refugee children with the tools they need to build a solid educational foundation and, consequently, a more promising future.

Furthermore, the proposal recognizes the role of education in fostering resilience and empowerment among refugee children. By allowing them to move freely for educational purposes, the hope is that these children can break the cycle of displacement, poverty, and limited opportunities. Education becomes a means not only for personal growth but also for contributing positively to rebuilding their communities and, eventually, their home countries.

While the idea of granting UN citizenship to refugee children for educational mobility is optimistic, it is not without its challenges. The logistics of implementing such a system, including ensuring the safety and well-being of the children during their travels, need careful consideration. Additionally, global collaboration between nations and educational institutions is essential to create a network that supports the seamless integration of refugee children into various educational settings.

The proposal acknowledges that providing educational mobility to refugee children is an investment in the future – not just for the individuals involved but for the global community as a whole. The potential benefits include a more educated and skilled workforce, enhanced cultural exchange, and the cultivation of a generation of individuals with a deep understanding of diversity and resilience.

The proposal to grant UN citizenship to refugee children with the ability to move freely for education reflects a commitment to breaking down barriers and providing opportunities that transcend the challenges of displacement. By envisioning a world where borders do not confine educational mobility, the international community strives to empower refugee children with the tools they need to shape their destinies and contribute meaningfully to a more inclusive and interconnected global society.

The proposal to grant UN citizenship to refugee children, allowing them the freedom to move globally for education, is seen as a significant contribution to fostering world peace in our society. The underlying principle is that education, when made universally accessible and borderless, becomes a powerful instrument for promoting understanding, empathy, and collaboration across diverse cultures and backgrounds.

One key aspect of how this contributes to world peace is by addressing the root causes of conflict and displacement. Education has the potential to break the cycles of ignorance and intolerance that often fuel conflicts. By providing refugee children with the opportunity to receive quality education on a global scale, there is a hope that future generations will be better equipped to understand, respect, and embrace cultural differences. This, in turn, can contribute to mitigating the factors that lead to violence and displacement in the first place.

Moreover, the proposal aims to create a generation of global citizens who have experienced education in different parts of the world. This exposure to diverse perspectives fosters open-mindedness and promotes a sense of shared humanity. When individuals from varied backgrounds learn together, they build connections that transcend geopolitical boundaries, diminishing stereotypes and prejudices. In this way, the proposal lays the groundwork for a more interconnected and harmonious global society.

Education is also a powerful tool for empowering individuals, and empowered individuals are more likely to engage in constructive and peaceful activities. By providing refugee children with the means to access education globally, the proposal seeks to break the cycle of despair often associated with displacement. Education equips individuals with the skills and knowledge necessary to contribute positively to their communities and the world at large, fostering a sense of agency and purpose.

Furthermore, the proposal acknowledges the potential role of education in conflict resolution. By nurturing critical thinking skills, conflict resolution mechanisms, and a deep understanding of human rights, refugee children can become advocates for peace in their communities. The hope is that these individuals, armed with the values instilled through global education, will actively contribute to building peaceful societies and promoting dialogue over discord.

The interconnectedness fostered by the proposal is not limited to individuals alone but extends to nations and regions. When refugee children move freely for education, it encourages international collaboration in the field of education. Nations working together to support the educational mobility of these children create a shared commitment to peace and cooperation. This collaborative effort transcends political differences and contributes to the creation of a more interconnected and interdependent world.

The proposal to grant UN citizenship to refugee children for global educational mobility is envisioned as a meaningful step toward fostering world peace. By addressing the root causes of conflict through education, promoting cultural understanding, empowering individuals, and encouraging international collaboration, the proposal seeks to create a future generation that values peace and cooperation. Ultimately, the hope is that these efforts will contribute to building a more peaceful and harmonious global society where the potential for conflict is diminished and the bonds of shared humanity are strengthened.

In acknowledging the harsh realities of our world, where the specter of war looms persistently, it becomes evident that while we may not entirely eliminate the occurrence of armed conflicts, we possess the agency to manage human society with the collective pursuit of world peace as an intrinsic right. This argument rests on the premise that, despite the complexities and challenges inherent in international relations, we have the capacity to shape a global society where the emphasis is placed on diplomatic solutions, conflict resolution, and fostering cooperation.

First and foremost, recognizing the inevitability of conflicts allows us to approach the goal of world peace with pragmatism. Wars have been a part of human history, often fueled by a myriad of complex factors such as political disputes, economic inequalities, and cultural differences.

Instead of harboring the illusion of eradicating wars altogether, we can focus on developing robust mechanisms for managing conflicts when they arise. Diplomacy, dialogue, and international cooperation become essential tools in this pursuit, enabling nations to resolve disputes without resorting to armed conflict.

By acknowledging the right to world peace, we embrace the idea that individuals and communities have a fundamental entitlement to live in societies free from the ravages of war. This recognition encourages the establishment of international norms and institutions dedicated to conflict prevention, peacekeeping, and post-conflict reconstruction. Through a shared commitment to world peace, nations can work collaboratively to create a global environment where the causes of conflict are addressed proactively, reducing the likelihood of violent confrontations.

Moreover, managing human society with the right to world peace at its core necessitates a shift in mindset – a move away from a zero-sum approach to international relations. Cooperation and mutual understanding become paramount, and nations are encouraged to engage in dialogue to resolve disputes peacefully. International organizations, such as the United Nations, play a crucial role in fostering this cooperative spirit by providing a platform for nations to come together, discuss differences, and find common ground.

Education emerges as a powerful instrument in managing human society toward world peace. By promoting a global curriculum that emphasizes the values of tolerance, understanding, and conflict resolution, we can shape the perspectives of future generations. When individuals are equipped with the knowledge and skills necessary to navigate differences peacefully, the potential for conflict diminishes. The right to world peace is, therefore, linked to the right to quality education that fosters a culture of peace.

Additionally, the promotion of economic and social justice contributes significantly to the management of society with the aim of achieving world peace. Economic disparities often serve as catalysts for conflict, and addressing issues of poverty, inequality, and social injustice becomes a preventive measure against the outbreak of violence. By creating a more equitable global society, we lay the groundwork for stability and cooperation, reducing the root causes of conflicts.

While we may not have the means to entirely eradicate war from the human experience, we possess the agency to manage human society with the inherent right to world peace. This involves a multifaceted approach that includes diplomatic solutions, conflict prevention mechanisms, international cooperation, education, and the pursuit of economic and social justice. By championing the right to live in societies free from the ravages of war, we can collectively strive toward a world where conflicts are managed with a commitment to peace, fostering a more harmonious and cooperative global society.

Chapter 8: Conclusion

In putting pen to paper for this book, my motivation stems from the stark reality I witnessed—the profound infringement upon the basic human rights of innocent individuals during and post-war periods. It became evident to me that the cry for sustenance and water, akin to the needs of animals, is not enough. There is a crucial necessity for recognizing and fulfilling their human rights.

As I reflect on the pages preceding this one, the purpose of this book crystallizes. It stands as a testament to the imperative need for a paradigm shift in our collective conscience. We must extend our efforts beyond mere survival necessities and advocate for the entitlements that distinguish us as humans— rights that transcend the basic sustenance of food and water.

In grappling with the vivid memories of witnessing human suffering in the aftermath of war, a genuine conviction rattled within me. The indomitable spirit of humanity should not merely exist; it should thrive in an environment that upholds the principles of justice, dignity, and peace. This is the crux of my message—a call to action, an impassioned plea for the realization of human rights for all.

The narrative unfolded on these pages is not a detached account of events; rather, it is a visceral reaction to the glaring disparity between what is and what should be. In bearing witness to the violation of human rights, I felt compelled to raise my voice to become an advocate for those whose cries often go unheard.

It is a duty, not born out of choice but out of an inherent sense of responsibility to humanity.

The path that led me to document these experiences was paved with the faces of those who endured the unimaginable. The faces are etched with the pain of loss, the scars of conflict, and the resilience that defies the darkest circumstances. In these faces, the true narrative lies—the untold story of the human spirit yearning for justice and a chance at a life free from the shackles of oppression.

To articulate the essence of my endeavor, it is paramount to underscore the distinction between mere survival and a life lived in accordance with the ideals of a just and compassionate society. The journey encapsulated in these pages is a testament to the belief that humanity can aspire to greater heights—a belief grounded not in utopian ideals but in the fundamental understanding that every individual, irrespective of circumstance, is entitled to basic human rights.

The plea for world peace that resonates through these words is not an abstract concept but a pragmatic call to address the root causes of conflict and strife. It is a recognition that peace is not merely the absence of war but a state of affairs where justice prevails and the rights of every individual are safeguarded. It is an acknowledgment that the pursuit of peace requires collective action, transcending borders and ideologies for the greater good.

As I pen down these concluding thoughts, the weight of the responsibility I have shouldered becomes apparent. The responsibility to convey a simple truth—that the narrative of our world need not be one of perpetual discord and suffering.

Instead, it can be a narrative of resilience, compassion, and the unwavering commitment to uphold the dignity of every human being.

In a world often besieged by the complexities of geopolitics and conflicting interests, the simplicity of this message becomes its strength. It is a call to strip away the layers of rhetoric and political maneuvering and recognize the shared humanity that binds us all. It is a reminder that, at its core, the pursuit of an ideal human society is a pursuit of justice, equality, and the assurance that every person can live a life of dignity.

In concluding this chapter, my hope is that these words resonate not as a lofty ideal but as a pragmatic blueprint for action. The call for recognizing human rights, the plea for world peace, and the vision of an ideal human society are not mere aspirations. They are imperatives that demand our collective attention, dedication, and action.

The story told in this book is not an isolated narrative but a reflection of the shared human experience. As we navigate the complexities of our world, let us not lose sight of the simplicity of our shared humanity—the common thread that binds us all. And in embracing this shared humanity, may we find the strength and resolve to build a world where the violation of human rights becomes a relic of the past, and the echoes of peace reverberate through the collective consciousness of our global society.

In the course of this book, we've delved into the harsh realities that have plagued humanity for centuries — a cycle of violence, destruction, and the profound impact it has on our shared existence. From the annals of history to the present day, war has been a constant companion, tearing through the fabric of societies and leaving a trail of despair in its wake.

The roots of this perpetual conflict run deep, with people shedding the blood of the innocent without discernible cause. War, in its various forms, has become a relentless force, shaping the destiny of nations and eroding the foundations of human society. In our contemporary age, the specter of atomic, biological (as exemplified by the COVID-19 pandemic), and chemical warfare looms large. Additionally, the battleground has expanded into the realm of media, where narratives are weaponized to further fuel the flames of discord.

The repercussions of war extend far beyond the battlefield. One of the most poignant consequences is the refugee crisis — a stark testament to the human cost of conflict. Forced to flee their homes, refugees find themselves cast adrift in a sea of uncertainty, stripped of the most basic human rights. Wars not only displace people but also rob them of their dignity, reducing them to a stateless existence akin to animals, driven solely by the primal instinct for survival.

Within this dire context, we encounter the profound issue of human rights violations. In the middle of warfare, the rights that form the bedrock of our shared humanity are trampled upon. Refugees, grappling with the aftermath of conflict, face a harsh reality where their very existence is in jeopardy. The international community, recognizing the gravity of this situation, has sought to provide a semblance of hope through the establishment of legal frameworks.

The United Nations, an entity born out of the collective desire for global peace, plays a pivotal role in this narrative. Through the granting of UN citizenship, a legal lifeline is extended to those who have been displaced by the horrors of war. This recognition serves as a beacon of hope, promising a pathway toward a better future for those who have been marred by the brutalities of conflict.

Crucially, this legal acknowledgment extends beyond the immediate refugee to encompass their progeny. By ensuring that the children of refugees are afforded the right to move freely for education and the pursuit of a better life, the UN lays the groundwork for a more harmonious world. Education becomes a powerful tool, a means to break the shackles of generational suffering and forge a path toward a brighter tomorrow.

In this seemingly unending cycle of strife, granting UN citizenship emerges as a small yet significant step toward global healing. It is a testament to our collective recognition of the shared humanity that transcends borders and political ideologies. In providing a legal framework for the displaced, we strive to rebuild the shattered foundations of human society.

The vision encapsulated in the UN's actions is one of inclusivity and shared responsibility. It is a recognition that the scars of war extend far beyond the physical battlegrounds — they seep into the very fabric of our interconnected world. By affording refugees the dignity of legal recognition, we acknowledge their right to rebuild their lives and contribute to the collective human civilization.

The road to world peace is fraught with challenges, and the refugee crisis is a stark reminder of the work ahead. Yet, in the face of such adversity, the UN's commitment to granting legal status to those displaced by war is a glimmer of hope. It symbolizes our collective endeavor to move beyond the shadows of conflict and forge a path toward a more compassionate and equitable world.

In a world where differences in governance can sometimes lead to conflict, the idea of a uniform global constitution proposed by the United Nations (UN) has garnered attention. The notion behind it is simple: to establish a set of rules and principles that would apply equally to all countries, regardless of their developmental status or geographical location.

At the heart of this proposal lies the recognition that disparities in the strength and effectiveness of national constitutions can impact various aspects of society, including protecting human rights and preventing conflicts. Developed Western countries often boast robust and comprehensive constitutions, carefully crafted to safeguard the rights and liberties of their citizens. These constitutions serve as the cornerstone of their legal systems, providing a framework for governance and ensuring accountability of those in power.

In contrast, many developing Eastern countries struggle with weaker constitutional frameworks. These constitutions may lack clarity, fail to adequately protect fundamental rights, or be subject to frequent changes and instability. As a result, citizens in these nations may face greater vulnerabilities, with their rights at risk of being infringed upon by those in authority.

One of the primary arguments in favor of a uniform global constitution is its potential to bridge these gaps and promote a more equitable system of governance worldwide. By establishing a common set of standards and principles, the UN aims to ensure that all countries provide their citizens with minimum protection and uphold fundamental human rights. This would help to address disparities between strong and weak constitutions, creating a more level playing field for all nations.

Moreover, proponents of this idea argue that a uniform global constitution could contribute to preventing conflicts and promoting peace. By setting clear guidelines for exercising power and protecting individual freedoms, such a constitution could mitigate the risk of abuses by authoritarian regimes and reduce tensions between states. Fostering a shared commitment to the rule of law and democratic principles could help build trust and cooperation among nations.

However, the proposal for a uniform global constitution is not without its challenges and criticisms. Some argue that imposing a single set of rules on diverse nations with varying cultural, historical, and political contexts could be impractical or even harmful. They warn against the potential for cultural imperialism and the undermining of national sovereignty. Others question the feasibility of reaching a consensus on such a complex and far-reaching endeavor, given UN member states' divergent interests and priorities.

Despite these concerns, the idea of a uniform global constitution represents a bold vision for a more just and peaceful world order. While the road ahead may be fraught with obstacles, the principles of equality, justice, and human dignity underpin this proposal resonate deeply with people's aspirations everywhere. Whether or not it ultimately comes to fruition, the discussion surrounding a uniform global constitution serves as a reminder of the importance of striving toward greater harmony and cooperation on the global stage.

The proposal for a uniform global constitution by the United Nations seeks to address disparities in national constitutions and promote a more equitable system of governance worldwide. By establishing common standards for the protection of human rights and the rule of law, it aims to bridge the gap between strong and weak constitutions and contribute to the prevention of conflicts. While the idea faces challenges and criticisms, it reflects a shared commitment to the principles of equality, justice, and peace that transcend national boundaries. Whether or not it becomes a reality, the pursuit of a uniform global constitution reminds us of the importance of working toward a more just and harmonious world for all.

As we reflect on the core concepts discussed throughout this book — the ravages of war, the plight of refugees, and the pursuit of human rights — we are confronted with the stark reality of our shared existence. In the face of such challenges, the path to world peace may seem arduous, but it is a journey we must undertake with unwavering determination.

The concluding chapters of our exploration into war, refugees, human rights, and world peace leave us with a profound sense of responsibility. It is a call to action, a plea to set aside the differences that fuel conflict and, instead, strive for a world where the inherent dignity of every individual is upheld. In the legal recognition of refugees, we find a glimmer of hope — a step toward a future where the scars of war do not define us but rather serve as a testament to our collective resilience and capacity for compassion.

In concluding our exploration into the grim realities of war, the plight of refugees, the violation of human rights, and the hopeful pursuit of world peace, I feel compelled to share a personal reflection with you, the reader.

As I pen down these final words, it is not merely an academic exercise or a detached analysis of the world's struggles. It is a shared journey through the annals of human history, a tapestry woven with the threads of triumphs, tragedies, and the enduring spirit that connects us all.

The narratives within these pages are not distant tales; they are the echoes of our shared experiences as inhabitants of this fragile planet. The weight of the words is not lost on me, for each account of war's devastation, every story of a displaced refugee, and each violation of human rights is a stark reminder of the collective responsibility we bear.

In the middle of these harsh realities, however, there exists a glimmer of hope — a hope that is not born out of naivety but forged in the crucible of our shared humanity. With its commitment to granting legal status to refugees, the United Nations exemplifies a beacon of possibility in an often bleak landscape.

I share this not as a detached observer but as someone who envisions a world where war scars no longer dictate our shared destiny. The granting of UN citizenship is not just a legal formality; it is a lifeline extended to those who have faced the harshest trials that humanity can inflict upon itself.

As we navigate the complexities of a world scarred by conflict, let us not forget that change begins with us — the individuals who make up the intricate mosaic of global society. The concluding message is not a call for grand gestures or sweeping reforms but a plea for collective introspection and compassionate action.

In the face of a seemingly insurmountable challenge, the small steps, the incremental changes, pave the way for a brighter future. By acknowledging the rights of refugees and affording them the opportunity for education and a better life, we contribute to a narrative of resilience, redemption, and, ultimately, peace.

This is not the end but a beginning — a call to engage with the world in a manner that transcends borders and embraces our shared humanity. It is a reminder that, even in the face of adversity, we possess the power to shape a future where the bonds of understanding and cooperation replace the ravages of war.

In these concluding words, I extend an invitation to you, the reader, to reflect on the collective responsibility we bear. Let us not be passive observers but active participants in the ongoing narrative of human civilization. Together, we can strive toward a world where the notion of war as a common occurrence becomes a relic of the past, and the pursuit of peace becomes the driving force of our shared journey.